WHAT MAKES A MAN A CHRISTIAN?

St PAUL'S CHURCH
BUSHEY

Advent 1968.

WHAT MAKES A MAN
A CHRISTIAN?

by

TIMOTHY DUDLEY-SMITH

HODDER AND STOUGHTON

PRINTED IN GREAT BRITAIN FOR HODDER AND STOUGHTON LIMITED,
ST. PAUL'S HOUSE, WARWICK LANE, LONDON E.C.4, BY
HAZELL WATSON AND VINEY LIMITED, AYLESBURY, BUCKS

To my Godchildren

ELIZABETH, ANDREW, PETER,
TIMOTHY, CHRISTOPHER,
JENNY, *and* MARK

ACKNOWLEDGMENTS

Verses of Scripture quoted in this book from the Old Testament are, unless otherwise stated, from the Revised Standard Version of the Bible, copyrighted in 1946 and 1952. Verses from the New Testament are from the New English Bible, New Testament, reproduced by permission of the Oxford and Cambridge University Presses.

THIS IS NOT an ordinary book; it is a 'programmed text'. That is, it asks questions for you to consider, and depending on your answer it guides you to the next chunk of information, the next step in the chain of reasoning. You will find more about how to use a programmed text on page 7; but if you start reading at the words BEGIN HERE, which are the title of chapter one on page 3, the explanations will follow in their proper order.

You will find that it helps to have a Bible (or at least a New Testament) handy. In most places I have set out in full any biblical reference, but I have added some extra ones which there is not room to quote, and which must be looked up in the Bible. I have assumed that whoever reads this has *some idea* of the story of Christ's life, as described in the four Gospels, and accepts what they say about Him, even if your recollection is based on nothing more than scripture lessons at school.

I owe some readers, at least, an explanation of why I have adopted the method of the programmed text, which is more often used for such down-to-earth subjects as learning algebra, or how to play Bridge. Surely, some people will say, for a subject like *What makes a man a Christian?* the method has more drawbacks than it has advantages? I grant you that the drawbacks are formidable. If you notice an absence of grandeur, a lack of feeling and dimension in these pages, you must put that down to the method, and the writer, but not the theme. If you find the thinking of this book too cut-and-dried for your taste, there are plenty of others. I do not suggest that the way set forth in these pages is the only and exclusive way.

But I have chosen this method because, for many people, the trouble with religion is that it is all so vague, so 'woolly'. This woolliness often characterizes religious books, so that practical people find them merely confusing. Woolliness cannot survive the discipline of programming; this book is written in this way because I want to use this teaching method to answer bigger questions than occur in algebra or Bridge.

After all, Christianity is not something we make up and add to as we go on along. It is a 'revealed religion'—something that can be taught. The New Testament does offer propositions, answer questions, and indicate the steps by which a man may move towards Christian discipleship. I have tried to set out some of these in the pages that follow.

If this method does not help you, you will find some books suggested on page 85 that approach the subject from a different standpoint. I suggest you start with one of those instead—and if you do, this book will have done its work for you before you are past the Introduction!

CHAPTER ONE

BEGIN HERE!

THE MORNING RUSH-HOUR is nearly over. Already the sun is hot on the pavements of the Edgware Road, and spring scents from the park are fighting a losing battle with the diesel fumes. A well-dressed man in a flannel suit—its sharpness of cut suggests Fifth Avenue—stands quietly waiting near the corner of Oxford Street. He holds a notebook unobtrusively in his right hand.

Round the corner comes a city gentleman, whose appearance proclaims 'prosperous stockbroker' as clearly as if it were written on his slender briefcase. He hesitates for a moment, looking at his watch. The American approaches him:

'Excuse me, sir. My name is Gallup—you may have heard of me. I am over here conducting a little personal research into the views of the British public. Would you be willing to answer a question for the purposes of my survey?'

The stockbroker nods. 'Well?' he asks.

Dr. Gallup refers to his notebook and puts his question:

'Would you mind, sir, telling me what it is, in your opinion, that makes a man a Christian?'

The stockbroker's jaw drops a little—he had not bargained on a religious conversation so early in the morning. But he collects himself, thinks for a moment, and replies:

'You've stopped the right man, as a matter of fact. I think I may be able to help you. Been going to church all my life. Ought to know something about it—vicar's warden for the last eight years, as a matter of fact. What makes a man a Christian, eh? Well, I think I can tell you. A man who goes to his church regularly on a Sunday—not just Harvest Festival and the British Legion—and attends Holy Communion every so often, and says his prayers and that sort of thing—yes, and a man who does his duty when the plate comes round—well, that would be my definition of a Christian man today. Can't ask much more than that—and not so many Christians about by that standard either.'

A little pink in the face, he watches while Dr. Gallup records his final words, and thanks him for his answer. Then he hails a passing taxi, and thankfully regains his privacy.

Dr. Gallup continues to scan the passers-by. There are fewer of them now. A policeman crosses the road and walks in his direction. Like all good Americans, Dr. Gallup knows that if you want help in London, a policeman is the man to ask. He stops the constable, explains his purpose, and puts his question:

'Excuse me, Officer, may I ask you a question? Would you mind telling me what it is, in your opinion, that makes a man a Christian?'

The policeman blinks for a moment. One has the impression that in more rural surroundings he would have pushed back his helmet and scratched his head.

'A Christian, is it?' he says. 'I don't know that I can tell you much about that. You meet some funny people in my job—things go on round this neighbourhood you wouldn't hardly believe. Most days we've a load of trouble up at the station—it sickens you after a time. I think of it like this: you show me a straight-living, law-abiding chap, that does as he would be done by, and respects the rights of others—and I'll show you what I call a Christian. Fine words are all very well; church-going is right enough in its way; but in the end it's what you do in your everyday life that matters. A Christian to me is a clean-living man. We could do with a few more of them.

'But if it's religion you're interested in, well, you see those trees over there?—Hyde Park, that is. Just by there, on a soap-box as likely as not, you'll find a chap who does nothing else all day but talk religion. He's the one to ask. Only you'll need a bigger notebook by the time he's finished telling you.'

The policeman moves ponderously on and Dr. Gallup turns towards the park. He finds a small cluster of people dispersing; the speech is over for the moment. The orator is sitting on his box, shuffling his papers. Dr. Gallup explains his mission, and then puts his question again:

'Would you mind telling me, sir, what it is, in your opinion, that makes a man a Christian?'

'But that's just what I've been talking about all morning,' says the orator testily. 'If only you had come a little earlier you would have heard it. It's really too bad arriving at the end and asking me to go over it all again now.'

4

'Perhaps,' says Dr. Gallup persuasively, 'you could just indicate briefly the main outline . . . ?'

'Well,' says the orator, after a pause, 'of course the main thing is to *believe*. A Christian is a man who believes the right things. Believe properly and you can be a Christian today.'

Dr. Gallup's pencil skims across his notebook. 'What sort of things should a man believe if he wants to call himself a Christian?'

'He must believe the Bible,' says the orator firmly. 'That is, the two testaments. And he must believe the three creeds and the four gospels and the five Books of Moses—but look here, this is my own book on the subject, *A Thousand Things a Christian must Believe*. You'll see it's divided into chapters. You needn't believe them all, all at once. Try to read a page a day, and practise believing. That's what makes a fallen creature . . . (*the orator throws out his chest and draws himself to his full height*) . . . a Christian man.'

* * *

It is going to take a remarkable computer to reconcile the results of Dr. Gallup's morning's work. He has received three totally different answers to his question, 'What makes a man a Christian?' They are answers that, in various forms and combinations, have been given to that question for a long time now. Some, like the stockbroker, make Christian discipleship a matter of religious observance. A Christian, on his showing, is a man who regularly and devoutly performs the ceremonial actions of religion—who says his prayers and attends his church. A good many respectable people will probably feel that the stockbroker has the root of the matter in him. But the policeman thinks differently. He is not over-impressed with church-going. For him the heart of Christianity is to be found in a man's conduct of his ordinary affairs—the way he lives his life. 'Fine words are all very well,' says the policeman; and he has met a good many church-goers whose lives do not measure up to the standard he expects. For his part, the orator pays little attention to either of these viewpoints. Religion for him is not a matter mainly of the *code* by which a man orders his life; or of the *ceremonies* of his church; but of the hard facts of what he actually believes—his *creed*.

* * *

Which of them is right? Is any of them? This book will help you to discover the answers for yourself, from the teaching of Jesus Christ Himself. From this point onwards it is not an ordinary book which sets the facts before you as you might hear them at a public lecture. Instead, this book will help you to learn by asking you questions; and what it has to say to you will vary according to your answers. Like a personal tutor, it will lead you step by step, repeating what is necessary, explaining what you have not understood. By the end of this short book you will have your own—authoritative—answer to Dr. Gallup's question: 'What makes a man a Christian?'

THIS IS NOT AN ORDINARY BOOK

MOST OF THIS BOOK is not designed to be read page by page by page. Instead, at the end of most pages you will find a question for you to think about. Immediately below the question three or four possible answers are given, of which usually one is right. When you have thought about the question, you choose which you think is the right answer.

Against each of these possible answers is printed in heavy type a page-number from this book. When you have made your choice, turn to the page whose number is printed against your answer. Here you will be told whether that answer was right or wrong. If it was right (and there will usually be a short explanation of *why* it was right) you will find on the same page a new question, and three or four possible answers to that one—and, once again, each will have a page-number printed against it, to turn to when you have made your choice.

But if you choose an answer which is wrong, then when you turn to the page indicated, you will be told not only that this is the wrong answer, but *why* it is the wrong answer; and you will be referred back, that much wiser, to try the question again.

This is the principle on which teaching-machines work. It may *sound* complicated in these instructions; but after you have tried it for a page or two, you will find it very simple to use. This teaching principle means that you almost *compile your own individual textbook*, exactly suited to the questions you want to ask as the discussion proceeds. Familiar ground is covered in great leaps and bounds. But what you find new and hard to understand is taken slowly, in detail, and from a number of angles. Now turn to the next page and make a start.

8

CHAPTER TWO

WHICH WAS RIGHT?

CONSIDER THE FABLE of the stockbroker, the policeman and the
soap-box orator in the first chapter of this book. (If you have not
read it, do so now. Turn back to page 1 and read from there.)
Suppose Dr. Gallup had later come up to you and said, 'I have
these three answers, all different, from men I spoke to this morning. Which of them in your view is right?'
What is your answer?

The stockbroker, whose answer stressed church-going
and prayer?   **page 11**

The policeman, whose answer stressed behaviour and
right living?   **page 12**

The orator, whose answer stressed believing the right
things?   **page 14**

All of them were right, taken together?   **page 16**

None of them was right, taken together, or taken
separately?   **page 18**

YOU SHOULD NOT BE READING
THIS PAGE!

If you have just finished page 8, and are now reading this page, as though this were an ordinary book, please go back and re-read the instructions on page 7, which will explain how to use a book like this.

None of the answers to the questions anywhere else in this book refer you to this page (page 9). If you think you were referred here by your answer to a question, please check to see whether you misread the page you are meant to turn to now.

10

From page 19

Your answer is that in those four verses from Mark's Gospel, Jesus is preparing for his future work.

This is not really so.

Of course it is true that, since this was the very start of His teaching career, he was laying the foundation for what was to come after. In that sense, your answer might be right.

But we have seen (page 19) that for Jesus the long years of waiting at home, which was the real time of preparation, are now over. If you look at the possible answers again, you will see one that is a much better description of what our Lord was doing.

Go back to page 19 and try again.

11

From page 8

Your answer is that you agree with the stockbroker, whose reply to Dr. Gallup's question stressed church-going and prayer.

It sounds right, but I am afraid it is wrong.

Church-going and prayer, and many other Christian observances are good and important. It would be a poor kind of Christian life that tried to do without them. But they are not answers to the question Dr. Gallup asked : 'What is it that makes a man a Christian?'

Jesus Christ, you may remember, had some hard things to say to the Pharisees on this subject. The Pharisees were the respectable religious people of His day, and spent a lot of time in the Temple or synagogue (which was their church) and making long (and rather ostentatious) prayers. But Jesus called them 'hypocrites' ! He said to his hearers, 'When you pray, do not be like the hypocrites; they love to say their prayers standing up in synagogues and at the street-corners, for everyone to see them' Matthew 6.5). Their prayers did not mean anything in their hearts. They were done for show.

This is one reason why prayers and church-going (important though they are as *a part of the Christian life*) cannot be said *to make a man a Christian*. Any hypocrite can go to church and say prayers, without necessarily meaning any of it.

We must look for an answer that takes less notice of what a man is like in outward appearance and actions, and pays more attention to what he is really like in himself. The Bible warns us that, 'The Lord sees not as man sees; man looks on the outward appearance, but the Lord looks on the heart' (1 Samuel 16.7).

Go back to page 8 and try again

12

From page 8

Your answer is that you agree with the policeman, whose reply to Dr. Gallup's question stressed behaviour and right living.

It may surprise you very much that your answer is wrong. It will probably help you to consider again the form of Dr. Gallup's question: 'What is it that makes a man a Christian?' Nobody denies that good behaviour and right living is an important part of any Christian life. Certainly you can hardly claim to be a Christian unless your behaviour is modelled on a Christian standard. But right living by itself is not enough *to make a man a Christian*. Some of the nicest people you know, who make no claim to be Christians, and who, if you asked them, would deny that they are Christians, behave admirably and live rightly according to the policeman's standard. *But not according to God's standard.* None of us measures up to that—'all alike have sinned' (Romans 3.23) is the message of the New Testament. 'All our righteous deeds' (our *righteous* deeds, mark you) 'are like a polluted garment' (Isaiah 64.6) is the clear-cut warning of the Old Testament. The Authorized Version, more bluntly still, says they are like 'filthy rags'. We cannot escape the taint of sin, even in our best moments. Because of this the Bible tells us that we can contribute nothing towards our acceptance with God by our own attempts at righteous living. It reminds us that it was '. . . not for any good deeds of our own, but because he was merciful, [God] saved us . . .' (Titus 3.5).

Although every Christian will have a high standard of conduct (but even Christians will sometimes fall to temptations), good behaviour itself cannot make a man a Christian.

Go back to page 8 and try again

13

From page 19

Your answer is that in these four verses from Mark's Gospel, Jesus is beginning to make disciples.

That is perfectly correct. The time of preparation is over. Jesus here is talking very particularly, first to a crowd ('proclaiming the Gospel of God'—you don't 'proclaim' to individuals) and then, a little time after, to Simon and Andrew. Both the crowd, and the two fishermen, were listening to Jesus and learning from Him— and this is the dictionary definition of disciple—'one who attends upon another for the purpose of learning from him'. By His proclaiming to the crowd, and His call to the two brothers, Jesus was beginning to make disciples.

Now 'making disciples' is what we want to learn about. We cannot find better guidance on the subject of '*What makes a man a Christian?*' than to see Jesus Christ Himself making disciples (the first 'Christians' of all, even though the name had not then been coined).

Refer back to the actual words with which He began: here they are:

'The time has come; the kingdom of God is upon you; repent, and believe the Gospel' (Mark 1.15).

What is Jesus here telling his audience to do first? Never mind if you don't exactly understand all the words He uses. Compare the verse above with the answers below.

To repent, when the time comes? **page 17**

To make a start, by repenting here and now? **page 22**

To believe the Gospel and become members of the kingdom of God? **page 20**

14

From page 8

Your answer is that you agree with the orator, whose reply to Dr. Gallup's question stressed believing the right things.

This is not the right answer, but you could be on the right track. The Bible has a lot to say about the importance of what a man believes in his heart—Romans 10.10, for instance: 'For the faith that leads to righteousness is in the heart . . .' Certainly right belief is a very important part of Christian living. Consider Hebrews 11.6: 'Without faith it is impossible to please him [God]; for anyone who comes to God must believe that he exists and that he rewards those who search for him.'

But this answer is wrong, all the same, mainly because the orator did not trouble to distinguish what a man believes in his head from the faith of his heart. 'To believe the creed', in the sense of being able to give an academic assent, never made anyone a Christian. Many people believe the creed who make no attempt to follow Jesus Christ. 'You . . . believe that there is one God. Excellent !' wrote James. But he went on, 'The devils have faith like that, and it makes them tremble' (James 2.19). The devil could sign his name to all that the orator suggested, and so could many other people, *in whom such belief makes no real difference at all.*

More is needed to make a man a Christian than just believing the right things. Intellectual assent is not enough.

Go back to page 8 and try again

15

From page 19

Your answer is that in these four verses from Mark's Gospel, Jesus is starting to talk generally about religion.

This answer is not wholly wrong. Jesus *is* talking about religion. But what He has to say is anything but general. It is very urgent and particular. It comes at a particular *moment* ('The time has come'); it is addressed to the *needs* of His hearers and tells them to follow a particular *course of action*—to repent, to believe the Gospel, to come with Him.

In the light of this, you should find that one of the other answers is a better description of what Jesus is doing.

Go back to page 19 and try again

16

From page 8

Your answer is that, while none of the replies Dr. Gallup collected are enough by themselves, they provide the right answer if taken together.

In other words, to go to church, to pray, to observe the ceremonies of religion; to live rightly and do as you would be done by; to believe the Bible and the creeds—these things, taken together, make a man a Christian. This is your answer.

It sounds right, but it doesn't quite work in practice. Most of us can think of somebody who fulfils all these conditions—regular at church, faultless in conduct, orthodox in creed—and yet who is proud, selfish, self-righteous, and very far from the spirit of Jesus Christ.

Of course all these things are good and important. It would be an odd sort of Christian living that could manage without them. But they cannot be assembled together to make a man a Christian, any more than a chemist who has assembled the salts and acids that make up a human body can thereby make a man. The same thing is missing in both cases—LIFE ! And spiritual life does not come from our own efforts—our many prayers, our righteous living, our sincere believing. It comes only from Jesus Christ. 'I am life,' He said (John 11.25). 'I have come that men may have life' (John 10.10). Without Him, religious practices and beliefs are dead and lifeless. Religion itself is dead (and sometimes rotten) apart from the living touch of Christ. Even taken together, these replies are not enough. You will probably guess that they are not enough taken individually either; but if you are in any doubt at all it may help you to look at page 11 to see other reasons why church-going is not enough, at page 12 to see other reasons why good behaviour is not enough, and at page 14 to see other reasons why orthodox belief is not enough.

Then go back to page 8 and try again

From page 13

Your answer is that Jesus is telling His hearers, in Mark 1.15, that they must first repent, when the time comes.

Here is the verse again:

'Jesus came into Galilee proclaiming the Gospel of God: "The time has come; the kingdom of God is upon you; repent, and believe the Gospel" ' (Mark 1.14, 15).

Look at it again. Jesus is not here telling them to do anything *when the time comes*. He is making it as plain as He can that *the time of preparation is over* for Him (He has begun His teaching career); and *the time of waiting is over* for His hearers. Look at the words, 'The time has come.' If you used them in ordinary speech would you not mean NOW, AT ONCE, IMMEDIATELY? Jesus is certainly not telling them to repent *when the times comes*. The time *has* come.

Go back to page 13 and try again

18

From page 8

Your answer is that none of the replies Dr. Gallup received was right, taken together or taken separately.

This is correct. You probably reasoned that though all those things are good and important in their place (and it would be an odd sort of Christian life that could manage without them) yet it is all too easy to fulfil these conditions—to be regular at church, faultless in conduct, orthodox in creed—and in spite of all that to be proud, self-centred, self-righteous, and very far from the spirit of Jesus Christ. If you want to check back over this, you will find it worked out on page 16.

But if we are agreed that Dr. Gallup is still a long way from learning the secret of what makes a man a Christian, at least we are beginning to see that *religious observance, of whatever kind, is not necessarily the same as Christianity*. Christians practice all these things—church and prayers, decent living, right beliefs. It is not surprising that the onlooker should think that the secret of Christianity lies in these things. But of course it does not. The secret of Christianity—the secret of spiritual life—lies in Jesus Christ Himself. He said of Himself, 'I am the way; I am the truth and *I am life*' (John 14.6). We cannot do better than turn to consider His own teaching. Read now the story at the start of chapter three.

page 19

WHAT JESUS PREACHED

THERE ARE EIGHTEEN hidden years in the life of Jesus Christ. All that we are actually told of them is found in half a verse of St. Luke's Gospel: 'He . . . continued to be under their authority' (Luke 2.51). These words are written of Jesus at the age of twelve, when He had visited Jerusalem with His parents, and stayed behind to ask questions in the Temple. He was eventually found by them (after some anxious hours) and taken back to His home in Nazareth. There, says St. Luke, he 'continued to be under their authority'. He worked with Joseph in the carpenter's shop. No doubt He helped look after younger brothers and sisters. Some say that after Joseph's death He became the family bread-winner, until a younger brother could take over the business.

So for those eighteen years Jesus stayed quietly at Nazareth. He was no doubt preparing Himself for the days when He would travel and teach. And finally the day came when He left home, began to gather disciples, and started His crowded three-year ministry. Mark tells the story like this:

'After John had been arrested, Jesus came into Galilee proclaiming the Gospel of God: "The time has come; the kingdom of God is upon you; repent, and believe the Gospel."

'Jesus was walking by the shore of the sea of Galilee when he saw Simon and his brother Andrew on the lake at work with a casting-net; for they were fishermen. Jesus said to them. "Come with me, and I will make you fishers of men." And at once they left their nets and followed him' (Mark 1.14–18).

Read these verses from Mark's Gospel carefully, and then consider this question: What is Jesus doing in these paragraphs?

Preparing for His future work?   **page 10**
Beginning to makes disciples?   **page 13**
Starting to talk generally about religion?   **page 15**

20

From page 13

Your answer is that Jesus is telling His hearers, in Mark 1.15, that the first thing they need to do is to believe the Gospel and become members of the kingdom of God.

Here is the verse again:

'Jesus came into Galilee proclaiming the Gospel of God: "The time has come; the kingdom of God is upon you; repent, and believe the Gospel" ' (Mark 1.14, 15).

You have overlooked the important word 'first'.

You are quite right that Jesus is wanting His hearers to believe the Gospel and to become members of the kingdom of God, but this is not what He is telling them to do *first*. He is here putting before them the steps *by which* they may become members of the kingdom of God, and it is the *first* step that we are after. You will find one of the other answers gives a better description of what that first step is.

Go back to page 13 and try again

21

From page 22

Your answer is that when Jesus told His hearers to *repent*, He was telling them to change their minds.

Correct.

This is literally true. It is the exact meaning of the word. That is why repentance is more than looking back with sorrow on the past. If regret for the past is not linked with resolve for the future, then it is only *remorse*. 'Repentance' means a change of mind (as we should say today, a change of heart) that *both* makes us sorry for our sins now past, and also makes us resolve that with God's help things will be different in future. Repentance, in fact, is a change of heart about the sort of person that we want to be. As Jesus used the word here, linked with the kingdom of God, it naturally means a change of heart towards God. From this will come sorrow for the past, a turning away from sin, and confession to God and the prayer for His forgiveness. These are the fruits of true repentance—true change of heart. Nothing less is repentance at all.

But even while we repent, we realize that we cannot change ourselves. The mere fact that I *want* in future to be different has little more power to change my future, by itself, than the wish that I had been different in my past life has power to change the past. It is therefore only a beginning, but it is an essential one. It is the first step on the road that makes a man a Christian.

'Repent' is also a very revealing word. When Jesus told His hearers to repent it indicated something of their present condition in God's eyes.

Which of these did His use of the word imply?

That He was talking to notably wicked people?   **page 23**
That all who heard him were in need of God's
forgiveness?   **page 25**
That His hearers' first need was to look back with
sorrow on their past life?   **page 27**

22

From page 13

Your answer is that Jesus is telling His hearers, in Mark 1.15, to make a start by repenting here and now.

This is perfectly right. 'The time has come,' Jesus told them. There is no need of further waiting. The kingdom of God, which had often seemed to the men of His day as something remote and distant, a golden age in the unforeseeable future, is *upon them*, here and now. And Jesus adds in this single verse two instructions to His hearers, which will be steps towards the kingdom. They are the commands to repent, and to believe the Gospel. They can begin at once (for 'the time has come') and the first thing He requires of them is that they *'repent'*.

What does this word mean? What exactly is Jesus telling them to do?

To change their minds?   **page 21**
To look back with regret on their past failings?   **page 24**
To ask God's forgiveness?   **page 26**

23

From page 21

Your answer is that when Jesus used the word 'repent', it implied that He was talking to notably wicked people.

This is not really so. We like to think of some people as much better than others, and some much worse; but the New Testament does not make many comparisons of this sort at all. Much more often, it is able to prescribe the same remedy for everyone.

Jesus Christ taught that the hearts of *all* men are by nature sinful. If you asked Him where the evil of the world came from, He would tell you 'out of the hearts of men and women'.

'It is what comes out of a man that defiles him,' he said. 'For from inside, out of a man's heart, come evil thoughts, acts of fornication, of theft, murder, adultery, ruthless greed, and malice; fraud, indecency, envy, slander, arrogance, and folly; these evil things all come from inside, and they defile the man' (Mark 7.21–23).

This is His teaching, echoed all through the New Testament. Paul, in Romans 3.10, quotes approvingly from the Old Testament: 'There is no just man (the Authorized Version says 'no righteous man'), *not one.*' He says in verse 23, 'All alike have sinned.'

The truth is that one would only use the word 'repent' to a man who needed to be changed—a sinful man. *But that is exactly, by nature, the condition of us all.* 'Repent' is a word *all human beings need.*

These words from the first Epistle of John are often said at the beginning of a service in church:

'If we say that we have no sin, we deceive ourselves, and the truth is not in us' (1 John 1.8, AV).

A not-unusual comment is that those who say they have no sin may deceive themselves, but 'certainly won't deceive their neighbours'. Whatever your merits as a citizen, you, like me, are a sinner in the sight of God. If Jesus' hearers had been entirely people like yourself, He would still have started His sermon with the command, *'Repent'.*

Go back to page 21 and try again

24

From page 22

Your answer is that when Jesus told His hearers to 'repent', He was telling them to look back with regret on their past failings.

This is true, but it is not enough. Repentance is a word that looks in two directions, forward into the future, as well as backwards to the past. It must include regret for past failings, but it includes a great deal more besides. There is a better definition of it among the possible answers on page 22.

Go back to page 22 and try again

25

From page 21

Your answer is that when Jesus used the word 'repent', He implied that all who heard Him were in need of God's forgiveness.

Right. 'Repent' is a word that can rightly be used to any human being, because it is a word that properly addresses sinners; and that means all of us.

Repentance always reminds me of the man in the petrol advertisement, with his two heads facing in opposite directions as the car flashes past him : 'That's Shell—that was !' Repentance does look back to the past, with regret; but it must chiefly look forward to the future, with resolve : 'God helping me, things will be different.'

Of course, mere repentance by itself cannot deal with the problems of the past or of the future. It cannot by itself *confer* forgiveness. If I change my mind (repent) on the matter of a long record of theft (ill-temper, selfishness, what-have-you) that does not wipe out the record of my mis-spent past. It does not entitle me to forgiveness. My past sins are still on my own shoulders. I am still what the New Testament calls 'a sinner', even when I have repented.

And, of course, my repentance cannot guarantee that I shall do better in future, whatever my resolve. But it does prepare me for the next step on the road, which our Lord introduces close on the heels of repentance : 'Repent,' He said, *'and believe the Gospel.'*

Repentance means a willingness to be changed. It is in the Gospel that there lies the power to do it.

This subject introduces a new chapter.

Turn to page 29 and continue there

26

From page 22

Your answer is that when Jesus told His hearers to 'repent', He was telling them to ask God's forgiveness.

This is partly true, but it is not accurate enough. Repentance is the step before asking for forgiveness.

Certainly we often speak as though to 'repent' meant exactly the same as to ask God's forgiveness. But in fact *it is the condition of asking* (and so of receiving) the forgiveness of God. In Luke 17.3, where Jesus is telling His disciples always to forgive one another, you can see that repentance comes before forgiveness: 'If your brother wrongs you, rebuke him; and if he repents, forgive him.' The repentance must come first, and it opens the door for forgiveness to follow. It is the *condition* of forgiveness.

You will find one of the other answers gives a better definition of the word 'repent'.

Go back to page 22 and try again

27

From page 21

Your answer is that when Jesus used the word 'repent' He implied that what His hearers needed was to look back with sorrow on their past life.

This is true as far as it goes, but it does not go far enough. Repentance, as we have seen (page 21), means literally 'a change of heart'. It is much more than looking back with sorrow on the past—which is often nothing more than remorse. Repentance looks also to the future, and includes a resolve that with God's help things will be different in future. It is, as we have seen, a change of heart about the sort of person we wish to be, and not just a fruitless regret about the sort of person that in the past we have been.

Certainly Jesus intended, when He told men to repent, that they should examine their past life, with sorrow for their sins. It is only when we look squarely and diligently at our record that we begin to realize what we are like inside. Seen in their true light, our sins (the things we have actually done wrong) are the most convincing evidence of our sin (the condition of our heart that makes it easy to do wrong, hard to do right). Our sins take many forms; but the root problem is the same. We want to run our own lives, be king of our own castle, do without God (or cut Him down to a size that suits our convenience). This is our sinful condition, and we cannot change it by ourselves.

When Jesus told men to repent, He was not just asking for an acknowledgment that they might have done better in the past. He was challenging them about the present condition of their hearts.

Go back to page 21 and try again

28

From page 39

Your answer is that when the Bible speaks of death as the penalty of sin, it is saying that the spiritual part of us is dead already, because of our sin.

Yes, this is right.

St. Paul puts it most clearly when writing to the Ephesians, and again to the Colossians. He tells his hearers that they were once dead, and have since been brought to life!

'Time was when you were dead in your sins and wickedness, when you followed the evil ways of this present age . . . But God, rich in mercy, for the great love he bore us, brought us to life with Christ even when we were dead in our sins . . .' (Ephesians 2.1–5).

'And although you were dead because of your sins . . . he [God] has made you alive with Christ' (Colossians 2.13).

Paul is not talking of literal resurrection (in the way that Jesus raised Lazarus, for instance) but of how *the real person* (the spiritual being, housed in this present body) can be dead through sin although the body lives on. By 'dead' in this spiritual sense Paul means 'cut off from God', the source of all spiritual life.

This then is the link between sin and death. Our sin separates us from God, and to be cut off from Him is spiritual death. That is why Paul writes to the Romans: 'Sin pays a wage, and the wage is death.'

But you will recall that when setting forth 'the Gospel' (page 30) Paul declared how 'Christ died for our sins', and we have seen that this was in order that we should not die for them ourselves (page 39). This is the meaning of the phrases in the verses quoted on this page above, about being 'brought to life with Christ' and 'made alive with Christ'.

In the light of this, do you think it most accurate to say that Christ died for our sins as:

Our example?	**page 36**
Our substitute?	**page 41**
Our sacrifice?	**page 45**

29

From page 25

CHAPTER FOUR

GOOD NEWS!

REPENTANCE IS THE FIRST STEP on the road that makes a man a Christian. The second, according to our Lord's sermon, is equally clear-cut and definite: 'The time has come; the kingdom of God is upon you; repent, *and believe the Gospel*' (Mark 1.15).

At the time Jesus spoke these words, the central truth of what He calls 'the Gospel' was not something cut-and-dried, known about, established. Rather, it was *taking place* among His hearers. It was highly contemporary. Others would know it later as something settled, recognized and clearly defined, only because it was here being worked out on the soil of Galilee and Judea. The kingdom of God was indeed 'at hand'. Later, we find the words 'the Gospel' linked more and more firmly with the events of Good Friday and Easter Day—the cross and triumphant resurrection of Jesus Christ. These are at the heart of 'the Gospel' to the writers of the New Testament—Peter and Paul and John among them.

But this Gospel is always good news ('good news' is the literal meaning of the word) about what *Jesus Christ* has done. It is not a crucifixion, or even a resurrection, that is significant, but WHO IT WAS they crucified, and is now alive for evermore. It is not a religious system that matters, but who Christ is, and what He has accomplished. From our standpoint today, looking back on Christ's birth, life, death, resurrection and return to heaven, what is this 'Gospel' in which the Bible asks us to believe?

St. Paul, like ourselves, could look back upon these events for most of his life as part of history. For him (and who should know better?) the good news of the Gospel lay in what was accomplished through them. Here is part of his letter to the Christians at Corinth in which he defines the word:

'And now, my brothers, I must remind you of the gospel that I preached to you; the gospel which you received, on which you

Continued overleaf on page 30

have taken your stand, and which is now bringing you salvation . . .

'First and foremost, I handed on to you the facts which had been imparted to me: that Christ died for our sins, in accordance with the scriptures; that he was buried; that he was raised to life on the third day, according to the scriptures; and that he appeared to Cephas, and afterwards to the Twelve [i.e. the twelve apostles]. Then he appeared to over five hundred of our brothers at once, most of whom are still alive . . .' (1 Corinthians 15.1–6).

This is a very important statement for our purpose. Read it carefully, and decide whether you think Paul is stating that his Gospel—his good news— is found primarily:

In the plain facts of history?   **page 38**
In the interpretation rather than in facts?   **page 32**
In the facts and their interpretation together?   **page 35**

31

From page 35

Your answer is that when Paul speaks of our sins as the cause of
the cross, he is referring mainly to those sins in the Bible story
which led directly to our Lord's arrest and execution.

Your answer is wrong.

Paul, writing to Christians at Corinth, would not have called
these 'our sins'. The Corinthian Christians were not in Jerusalem
when Christ was crucified.

It is of course true that the sins of the priests, of Judas and
Pilate, and the betrayal of the disciples, *did* contribute to Christ's
arrest and execution. But if you will read St. Paul's words again
(you will find them on page 30) I think you will see that this is
not what he is writing about.

Go back to page 35 and try again

32

From page 30

Your answer is that Paul is stating in the opening verses of
1 Corinthians 15 that his Gospel is found in the *interpretation*,
rather than in the facts of the events he recounts.

This answer cannot be right because the interpretation is value-
less unless the facts are true.

Here are Paul's words again :

'First and foremost, I handed on to you the facts which had
been imparted to me : that Christ died for our sins, in accordance
with the scriptures; that he was buried; that he was raised to life
on the third day, according to the scriptures; and that he
appeared . . .'

The interpretation, found in the words 'for our sins', is of the
first importance.* Without it, Paul might be recording only a
great tragedy of a promising life cut short by cruel men. Christ's
death *if it were only an accident of circumstances* could never be
'good news'. So you are right in thinking that the interpretation
is important.

But the answer you chose has this great weakness—that it
drives a wedge between the facts and their meaning. It concen-
trates on the meaning *rather than the facts*.

We must have both. These things actually happened. We have
the meaning only because we have the fact. Look at how much
of Paul's words above are taken up with historical fact—but the
interpretation is there as well.

Go back to page 30 and try again

---

* We need not concern ourselves here with whether the words 'in
accordance with the scriptures' are primarily fact or primarily interpretation.

33

From *page 35*

Your answer is that, when Paul speaks of our sins as the cause of the cross, he is referring mainly to the fact that if we ourselves had been placed in the same position as the priests, or Judas, or the disciples, or Pilate, we might well have done no better than they did.

That is not the right answer. I do not deny for a moment that we might have failed in the same ways (or worse ones) than all the people in the sorry list above. But in fact we did not. We did not have the opportunity. And you cannot include among 'our sins' the sins we might have committed in certain circumstances which never in fact happened to us.

It is true that *we are all*, through our sins, the cause of the cross; and if this is what you were feeling after, it shows you are on the right track. But Paul here is writing in a different and deeper sense.

Go back to page 35 and try again

34

From page 39

Your answer is that when the Bible speaks of death as the penalty of sin, it is saying that to choose sin is to court an early grave.

No, this is not right. To begin with, no mention is made of time at all (it is of course true that the more dissipated kinds of sin can shorten a man's life, but the Bible never suggests that sins of the body are worse than other sins). And in experience, the godless man often lives to a ripe old age while 'the good die young'. There is a slightly spine-chilling proverb which says, 'The mills of God grind slowly, but they grind exceeding small'— God's judgment on sin is none the less certain for not being in a hurry. Indeed, St. Peter makes the point in his second letter (2 Peter 3.9) that God is often patient with those in spiritual need 'because it is not his will for any to be lost, but for all to come to repentance'.

The age at which a man dies is no index of his moral goodness. This is not what the Bible is saying in linking death with sin.

Go back to page 39 and try again

35

From page 30

Your answer is that Paul is stating in the opening verse of 1 Corinthians 15 that his Gospel is found both in the facts of history,
and in the interpretation of these facts, taken together.

You are perfectly right.

Most of what Paul states to be his Gospel in these verses is an
account of plain unvarnished historical truth (the twice-repeated
'in accordance with the scriptures', though important in its place,
need not detain us here. It refers to Old Testament prophecies
about the cross—for instance, Isaiah, chapter 53). But there are
three vitally important words of interpretation—the words *'for
our sins'*. They turn a tragedy into a triumph. Without them, the
cross of Jesus could never be called 'good news'.

But they are not easy words to interpret accurately. When Paul
speaks of our sins as the cause of the cross, is he referring mainly
to:

Those sins which led directly to our Lord's arrest and
execution—the hatred of the priests, the betrayal of
Judas, the desertion of the disciples, the weakness of
Pilate? * **page 31**

The fact that if we ourselves had been placed in the
same position as the priests, or Judas, or the disciples,
or Pilate, we might well have done no better than they
did? **page 33**

The fact that, if Christ had not died 'for our sins' we
should have had to die for them ourselves? **page 39**

* If you are not clear about what happened, or the parts played in
the story by these individuals, you are advised to read carefully one or
more of the accounts in the Gospels of Matthew, Mark, Luke, and
John.

36

From page 28

Your answer is that, choosing from the three words 'example', 'substitute', 'sacrifice', you think it most accurate to say that Christ died for our sins as our example.

Think again ! It is true that the Bible holds up to us the example of Jesus Christ as a model for us to follow when called upon to suffer—but it only does so in one or two isolated instances.

And even though we may draw inspiration from the supreme example of our Lord's patience under suffering, the thought that He was being an example to us offers no clue as to any way in which His example could take away our sins.

Go back to page 28 and try again

From page 46

Your answer is that the command to 'believe the Gospel' in Mark 1.15 is an invitation to a moral choice.

It is impossible to say that you are wrong; but it is not the best answer of the three suggested.

Certainly if we do believe the Gospel, most of us are going to be faced with a good many moral choices. In particular, if we believe that 'Christ died for our sins' (which we have seen to be a very important part of the Gospel message) then we cannot lightly go on committing them.To 'believe the Gospel' is to accept a very different standard of behaviour from the current standards of most human societies. In that sense, belief in the Gospel involves a moral choice. But this is not the *essence* of believing. There is an answer that goes deeper.

Go back to page 46 and try again

38

From page 30

Your answer is that Paul is stating in the opening verses of 1 Corinthians 15 that his Gospel is found in the plain facts of history.

Your answer is not quite right, though it certainly sounds as if it might be.

Here are Paul's words again:

> 'First and foremost, I handed on to you the facts which had been imparted to me: that Christ died for our sins, in accordance with the scriptures; that he was buried; that he was raised to life on the third day, according to the scriptures; and that he appeared . . .'

They include, alongside the historical facts, an interpretation of Christ's death—that it was *for our sins*.* The recognition that we were involved in some way in Christ's death is a vital part of Paul's Gospel—and of the Christian Gospel in every age. History records that Jesus died on a cross. The Gospel adds that it was *for our sins*. The facts of history, left to themselves, sound like bad news rather than good—the cruel and unjust death of the best man ever, on what might well be known to future generations as Black Friday. But the Gospel declares that by this death the problem of our sins can be dealt with . . . and that is why the Gospel is 'good news'.

Go back to page 30 and try again

---

* It is true that 'in accordance with the scriptures' is also in some ways an interpretation as well as a fact, but that need not concern us here.

39

From page 35

Your answer is that when Paul speaks of our sins as the cause of the cross, he is referring mainly to the fact that if Christ had not died 'for our sins' we should have had to die for them ourselves.

You are quite right. We are getting to the heart of the Gospel.

You sometimes hear people talk as though Christ's death was a tragic accident—that He was the victim of circumstances that got beyond His control. Nothing could be further from the truth. Throughout the story of His arrest, trials, and judgment, Jesus Christ dominates the scene. In the Upper Room, well aware that Judas is plotting against Him, Jesus carefully informs him that they are soon leaving for the lonely garden where the arrest can be accomplished without fuss and publicity. On trial before Pilate, Jesus tells the Roman Governor: 'You would have no power over me, unless it had been given you from above.' When Peter started fighting to defend Him, Jesus told him, 'Put up your sword . . . Do you suppose that I cannot appeal to my Father, who would at once send to my aid more than twelve legions of angels? But how then could the scriptures be fulfilled, which say that this must be?' (Matthew 26.52–54). His own position in all this He made very plain to His followers beforehand: 'No man has robbed me of it [my life]; I am laying it down of my own freewill. I have the right to lay it down, and I have the right to receive it back again' (John 10.18).

The fact is that Christ died willingly—deliberately—because if He had not died 'for our sins' we should have had to die for them ourselves. He did it out of love.

The Bible often speaks of death as the penalty of sin (for example, in Romans 6.23, 'Sin pays a wage, and the wage is death'). When it does so, do you think it is saying that:

To choose sin is to court an early grave? **page 34**

The spiritual part of us is dead already, because of our sin? **page 28**

Those who sin most find death most bitter when it comes? **page 47**

Your answer is that, choosing from the three words 'example', 'substitute', 'sacrifice', you think it most accurate to say that Christ died for our sins as our substitute.

This is correct, though it would not be wholly wrong to have chosen 'sacrifice' (see page 45).

Of course, the idea that Jesus Christ died *in my place, as my substitute*, does not exhaust the meaning of the cross. He made there a great sacrifice; he gave a supreme example of patience under suffering. We have already seen that 'Christ died for our sins' is the message of the New Testament writers—of Paul in just those words in 1 Corinthians 15.3; Peter in 1 Peter 3.18, 'Christ also died for our sins once and for all'; of John in 1 John 3.5, 'Christ appeared, as you know, to do away with sins.' The writer to the Hebrews says; 'Christ was offered once to bear the burden of men's sins . . .' (Hebrews 9.28) and Peter has also this vivid phrase : 'In his own person, he carried our sins to the gallows . . . By his wounds you have been healed . . .' (1 Peter 2.24).

Putting this evidence together, the plain teaching of the Bible (in the Old Testament, with its lessons of sacrifice, and in the New with its explanations of that first Good Friday) we find that Christ is our Saviour because He is our sin-bearer. When I should have been condemned to die, He took my place—'stood in for me' as we say—and accepted in Himself the consequences of my sin.

This is the good news of the Gospel, when it is coupled with the fact of Christ's resurrection from the dead. What matters is not the exact way in which it was accomplished (human minds will never fully understand or explain all that was involved in the death of the Son of God) but that beyond doubt, for those who will have it so, Jesus Christ died 'for our sins' so that we should not have to die for them ourselves.

We need to add that the Bible is at pains not to suggest that Christ's death was in any way a means to appease an angry God. St. Paul reminds us that, 'From first to last this has been the work of God. He has reconciled us men to himself through Christ . . . What I mean is, that God was in Christ reconciling the world to himself, no longer holding men's misdeeds against them . . .' (2

Continued overleaf on page 42

Corinthians 5.18,19). And again, this is made plain in Ephesians
2.4 & 5. 'But God, rich in mercy, for the great love he bore us,
brought us to life with Christ even when we were dead in our
sins.'

In the cross, where Jesus died 'for our sins' we see most plainly
the love and mercy of God towards us.

This is the first and most important part of Paul's description
of 'The Gospel'. We move on to the rest of his account.

Here again, then, is Paul's summary of what he held to be the
Gospel: you will find the whole of the passage in 1 Corinthians
15.

> 'And now, my brothers, I must remind you of the gospel that
> I preached to you; the gospel which you received . . .
>
> 'First and foremost, I handed on to you the facts which had
> been imparted to me: that Christ died for our sins, in accordance
> with the scriptures; that he was buried; that he was raised to
> life on the third day, according to the scriptures; and that he
> appeared to Cephas, and afterwards to the Twelve. Then he
> appeared to over five hundred of our brothers at once . . .'

We have been thinking so far of the first part of this statement
of the Christian Gospel—'that Christ died for our sins, in accordance with the scriptures'. The last phrase, 'in accordance with
the scriptures', we have had to disregard, because there is no room
in a book of this size to go into the Old Testament record, which
Christ by His coming fulfilled. A good single example can be
seen in Isaiah, chapter 53.

Re-reading the statement of the Gospel above, there are three
other items which Paul mentions as together composing the
account committed to him. 'Christ died for our sins' has come
first, and we have examined it. In order of importance, which of
these three would you place next?

That He was buried . . . ?   **page 44**
That He was raised to life . . .?   **page 46**
That He appeared . . .?   **page 40**

43

From page 46

Your answer is that the command to 'believe the Gospel' in Mark 1.15 is an invitation to an intellectual exercise.

No. This is not correct. Indeed, if you will read over again the answer at the top of this page, I think you will feel that it sounds wrong from the start.

The difficulty springs from the word 'believe', which we use in a great many senses, often very differently from the sense in which it is used in the command to 'believe the Gospel'. When we say 'believe' we often are asking simply an assent of the mind; and even here we use the word remarkably lightly. We say not only, 'I believe men should obey conscience' (an affirmation which, if it means anything, probably means a lot to us), but also, 'I believe it is going to rain', which is only another way of saying that we cannot be sure!

The Bible tells us there is no certain value in our mere opinions, in intellectual assent to the facts of the faith. We saw earlier (page 14) that 'the devils have faith like that (James 2.19). Of course any true belief must include sincere intellectual assent, but it must not stop there.

Go back to page 46 and try again

From page 42

Your answer is that in Paul's statement of the Gospel, next in importance to the fact that 'Christ died for our sins' is the fact that He was buried.

I cannot agree with you. It is a matter of opinion, but I think that one of the others is out of all proportion more important.

At the same time, the fact that Christ was buried *is* part of the very brief and condensed statement of the Gospel that Paul records. It must be important, even if not of supreme importance. I believe Paul insists on it because it bears witness to the fact that Jesus actually did die. Many theories have grown up to disprove the resurrection of Christ—none of them notably successful—and among them the suggestion that Jesus was never dead at all. He fainted on the cross, the theory goes, was taken down, and revived in the coolness of the tomb (which was a rock-hewn cave, and not a grave dug in the earth).

The weaknesses of this theory have always prevented it from gaining serious acceptance—a crucified body, pierced by a spear, was in no shape to revive under exposure, without benefit of medical attention. But the fact that Jesus was buried means that (in Paul's day) there were plenty of eye-witnesses who could vouch for the fact that the body had been placed in a cave, which was then sealed and guarded. It was a dead body, carefully watched. But in two days' time it had gone. Christians believe that Jesus was risen, as He said He would be, having been really dead. He was dead and *buried* and is alive again. The New Testament is consequently able to say of Him that He has 'broken the power of death' (2 Timothy 1.10).

Go back to page 42 and try again

From page 28

Your answer is that, choosing from the three words 'example', 'substitute,' 'sacrifice', you think it most accurate to say that Christ died for our sins as our sacrifice.

Sacrifice, yes; but *our* sacrifice, no. We did not offer Him. He offered Himself for us.

It would be entirely accurate to talk of *His* sacrifice, because He made it. As we have seen (page 39) Jesus went willingly to the cross. He could have escaped it if He had chosen. He went there to die for sins—not His own, for He had none, but ours. He sacrificed Himself for us. He died an agonizing death, and endured the torments of separation from God His Father, so that we need never know such separation.

Faced with this sacrifice, words fail. But two things should be noted. First, as we have seen, it was a willing sacrifice. Secondly, it accomplished its purpose. In the Communion service, Christ is spoken of as having made, by His death for us, 'a full, perfect, and sufficient sacrifice' for the sins of the whole world.

He was our sacrifice in the sense that He sacrificed Himself for our sakes, and your answer would not therefore count against you if this was an examination. But of the three alternatives, there is one which fits the form of the question even better.

Go back to page 28 and try again

46

From page 42

Your answer is that in Paul's statement of the Gospel, next in importance to the fact that 'Christ died for our sins' is the fact that He was raised to life ...

You are absolutely right. My only doubt would be whether it was really possible to separate the two things at all and say that one is 'more important' than the other. In the New Testament, Christ's death and resurrection go together, both in the facts of history, and in the teaching of the apostles. The fact that He was buried has its own importance (turn to page 44 if you want to know more) and so does the fact that He was seen (page 40), but far more important is the triumphant fact that He rose from the dead, and is living still.

Not only does this mean that what He died to win—the forgiveness of our sins, the offer of a new life—is assured and achieved. It means also that Christ is *alive today*. Christians do not worship a Son of God who met His final end (no matter how heroically) on a gallows nineteen hundred years ago: they worship a risen, living, and victorious Lord and Saviour, whose promise to His followers is this: 'Be assured, I am with you always, to the end of time' (Matthew 28.20).

In briefest outline this is the New Testament Gospel. What are we to make of the command to 'believe' it (Mark 1.15)? Is it, do you suppose, an invitation to:

A practical experiment?   **page 48**
A moral choice?   **page 37**
An intellectual exercise?   **page 43**

47

From page 39

Your answer is that when the Bible speaks of death as the penalty of sin, it is saying that those who sin most find death most bitter when it comes.

No, this is not primarily what the Bible means when it links death with sin (as in Romans 6.23, 'Sin pays a wage, and the wage is death'). It is true that for the sinner, death is bitter; for 'the sting of death is sin' (1 Corinthians 15.56)—but in the light of this verse what should worry us is not the fact of dying, but that death brings us to judgment, with our sins unforgiven. In that sense, the bitterness of death is related to the sins of this life.

The Bible is not as ready as we are to grade men into finely-distinguished groupings. Its message is that *all* men are sinners and under judgment, and that *all men* will find death bitter, because judgment awaits them—and not only judgment, but condemnation. St. Paul, writing to the Romans, tells them that 'All alike have sinned'; or as the Authorized Version puts it, 'there is no difference, for all have sinned' (Romans 3.23).

When the Bible talks of death as the penalty of sin, it is speaking of something that affects us all equally.

Go back to page 39 and try again

48

From page 46

Your answer is that the command to 'believe the Gospel' in Mark 1.15 is an invitation, not so much to a moral choice or an intellectual exercise, as to a practical experiment.

You are quite right. It will include moral choices (and there is more about this on page 37 if you want it), just as it must include sincere intellectual assent (page 43), but the Gospel is more than a set of mere obligations, and more than a collection of academic propositions. St Paul, in the résumé of the Gospel which we have considered from 1 Corinthian 15.3-6, says that he was 'handing on the facts' to his Corinthian readers. What these facts demand is practical experiment—a verdict that affects not just our mind, or even our will, but *the whole person*—which is why the Bible speaks so often in terms of 'the heart', the core or centre of our being, the real me.

In short, the invitation to 'believe the Gospel' is not so much 'accept the facts' as 'trust the Person'. If Jesus Christ has really made possible our forgiveness (and more, our deliverance from the power of evil over us), and defeated death, and risen to new life, in which He can be our Companion, then these stupendous truths demand more from us than 'I quite agree' or 'I don't dispute it'. They demand a total response—which the Bible calls faith. The invitation to 'believe the Gospel' is a call to faith in Jesus Christ, who is not just a figure of history (though He is that) but our living and real contemporary.

And to put our faith in Christ is nothing less than a practical experiment, the gateway to Christian experience. If repentance is the first step on the road that makes a man a Christian, faith is the second.

*   *   *

This is the point at which to look again over the ground we have already covered, and to see the progress that we are making towards the biblical answer to Dr. Gallup's question: 'What makes a man a Christian?'

Turn now to the next chapter, headed PROGRESS REPORT.
(Page 49)

CHAPTER FIVE

PROGRESS REPORT

WHAT MAKES A MAN A CHRISTIAN? We have seen so far that none of the three answers Dr. Gallup received is wholly satisfactory, nor even all three taken together. To be a Christian is something more than to follow the right ceremonies, code, and creed. In search of this 'something more' we began to study the first recorded sermon of our Lord Jesus Christ. 'The time has come; the kingdom of God is upon you; repent, and believe the Gospel.'

We examined with some care the meaning of the word 'repent', distinguishing it from mere remorse, and finding in it the root meaning of 'change of heart'. We saw that repentance includes both regret and resolve: *regret* for things that have been wrong in the past; and *resolve* that, for the future, God helping us, things will be different. But that little clause 'God helping us' is of the first importance. Repentance by itself has no dynamic of its own, to ensure that what it regrets does not re-occur, or what it resolves is ever translated into practice.

We also found in repentance the first step towards forgiveness for the past, in that it is the condition of asking—or at least of receiving—the forgiveness that God offers to those who truly repent.

From our study of repentance, we moved on to the next command of our Lord in His sermon, which was: 'Believe the Gospel.' From 1 Corinthians we examined Paul's brief and concise résumé of the essentials of 'the Gospel' as he preached it; and saw that it was first and foremost a clear-cut proclamation of the 'good news' that Christ died for our sins. Once this is realized, that tragedy of Good Friday becomes a triumph. Jesus was not a victim of circumstance, but a willing sacrifice, achieving by the costly way of the cross what could be achieved in no other way—the forgiveness of our sins. We considered strands of evidence from a number of New Testament writers, all concerned to reiterate this single truth; and while recognizing that no human description is going to be sufficient fully to explain the cross, we agreed that Christ

Continued overleaf on page 50

died as more than our example; indeed, He died that we might not have to die; in a word He took our place, and was our substitute.

But Paul's Gospel is not exhausted by the good news that Christ bore our sins. It adds the valuable evidence that the Lord was buried; and passes then to the supreme assertion that the grave could not hold Him, and that He rose from the dead, and was seen by His friends. From the rest of the New Testament we can fill out Paul's brief statement, and say that the truth of the Gospel includes the triumph of Christ over death and sin, His victorious resurrection, witnessed to by many appearances to His friends, before His return to 'the right hand of Majesty on high'. Even so, He is not taken from us; but His followers have His promise, 'be assured, I am with you always, to the end of time' (Matthew 28.20).

Finally in the last section we rejected the idea that the word 'believe' in this context was limited to mere intellectual assent. Instead, we saw in it our Lord's invitation to an act and attitude of faith or trust – comparable to the trust of a patient in his doctor—with the most far-reaching consequences.

We now turn to the next section, which examines the results of our repenting and believing, and what must follow from them. Here, by the way of introduction, is St. Mark's account of the calling of Simon and Andrew, immediately following the verses quoted above. We have met them before in this book already (page 19).

'Jesus was walking by the shore of the Sea of Galilee when he saw Simon and his brother Andrew on the lake at work with a casting-net; for they were fishermen. Jesus said to them, "Come with me, and I will make you fishers of men." And at once they left their nets and followed him' (Mark 1.16–18).

Looking carefully at this call to the two brothers, would you describe it as :

A call to repentance?   **page 53**
A call to belief?   **page 56**
A call to commitment?   **page 59**

51

From page 59

Your answer is that the proper order of the three steps to Christ we have been considering is faith, repentance, commitment.

No, you are wrong. When you find which of the three suggestions is the right answer, that will tell you why you are wrong.

But if on re-reading the answer you chose (set out above), you cannot see for yourself that something is amiss, then you may be well advised to do a swift recap of your own.* One of the words above is in its right place, and two are transposed. You can re-read the section dealing with the transposed words if you go back to page 13. In a book of this nature, to go back 40 pages does not mean that you have 40 pages to re-read. You will probably not have read for long before your mistake will dawn on you; and since you ought to be able to turn at once to the right answer at the foot of each page, your progress will be very rapid.

This will be a much better plan, if you want to master the subject of this book, than merely returning to page 59 and choosing one of the two other suggestions at random.

When you are ready, go back to page 59 and try again

* Particularly if by any chance this is your second attempt at the question, because your first was wrong as well.

53

From page 50

Your answer is that the call to the two brothers in Mark 1.17, 'Come with me, and I will make you fishers of men', is a call to repentance.

No, this is not the best answer. There may be some truth in it, since however convenient it is in theory to separate out the component parts of Christian experience, and say, 'This was repentance' or 'This was faith', real life is never quite as neat and tidy. Things happen simultaneously. More than one cause is at work to produce a particular result.

Nevertheless, this is not a call directed to win from the brothers a change of heart about themselves—to bring about regret for their past or resolve for their future which is a rough and ready definition of repentance. It presupposes that such resolve is already there, and invites the fishermen to translate it into action.

There is a better answer among the three suggested.

Go back to page 50 and try again

54

From page 59

Your answer is that the proper order of these three steps to Christ we have been considering is commitment, repentance, faith.

No, this is wrong. When you find out which of the three suggestions is the right answer, that will tell you why you are wrong.

But if on re-reading the answer you chose (set out above), you cannot see for yourself that something is amiss, then you may be well advised to do a swift recap on your own.* Two of the words above are in their right relation to each other, and one is in quite the wrong place. You can re-read the section dealing with this word if you go back to page 49, start chapter five again, and go on from there.

This will be a much better plan, if you want to master the subject of this book, than merely returning to page 59 and choosing one of the two other suggestions at random.

When you are ready, go back to page 59 and try again

* Particularly if, by any chance, this is your second attempt at the question, because your first was wrong as well.

55

From page 69

Your answer is that by the words 'eternal life' the Bible means primarily life after death, in heaven.

No, it does not primarily mean that, though it includes it. Eternal life is not interrupted by death in the way that physical life is; it continues after death in heaven. But it is not restricted to such life after death.

If you care to look at 1 John 5.13 you will read there, 'This letter is to assure you that you have eternal life . . .' Eternal life can therefore be a present possession.

Go back to page 69 and try again

56

From page 50

Your answer is that the call to the two brothers in Mark 1.17, 'Come with me, and I will make you fishers of men', is a call to belief.

No, this is not the best answer, though it is a more likely choice than one of the others. We have seen that the belief spoken of here is not mere intellectual assent to the facts, but a total response of our whole person to the Person of Jesus Christ. Certainly when we find the brothers responding to this call and leaving their nets and following Jesus, they are exercising faith.

But it is not splitting hairs to say that the faith was there already. They were ready to respond when the call came. They already had enough faith in Jesus to come when He called them. What they are doing here is *acting on their faith*, stepping out into the unknown in response to Christ's invitation. Metaphorically at least they are crossing a Rubicon, turning their back on their former pattern of life, and making a new start with Christ.

There is a better word for this among the three suggestions offered.

Go back to page 50 and try again

57

From page 62

Your answer is that you find the idea of commitment most clearly implied in the title 'The Son of God'.

No, this is not the obvious choice. It is true that if anyone can command our allegiance (and commitment is the step of giving unqualified allegiance) it ought to be God Himself. But we know in fact that it does not work like this in practice—and if it does not work with God, then why should it with 'The Son of God'?

There is a title among the three suggested which speaks more clearly still of the idea of commitment.

Go back to page 62 and try again

58

From page 65

Your answer is that when Jesus called Simon and Andrew to follow Him, He told them that He wished to teach them something.

No, this is not the right answer.

Obviously Jesus had much to teach them since He called them to be His disciples, and the word 'disciple' means 'learner' or 'pupil'. But He Himself did not at this moment speak to them about learning and teaching. He told them at the time that He was calling them for another reason.

Go back to page 65 and try again

From page 50

Your answer is that the call to the two brothers in Mark 1.17, 'Come with me, and I will make you fishers of men', is a call to commitment.

Perfectly right. We do not know enough about the inner workings of the hearts of either of them to be sure that other answers are totally wrong. But what they are doing when they leave their father and their boats to go with Jesus is better described in terms of *commitment* than in terms of repentance or even belief. This is a new subject and had better have a new chapter.

CHAPTER SIX

COMMITMENT

COMMITMENT is not a biblical word. It seems not to have been needed in days before the word 'believe' had been so emptied of content as to mean primarily mere assent. But today 'commitment' expresses a key part of what makes a man a Christian. Not only must he repent; not only must he have a living faith in Jesus Christ; but he must make an actual decisive step of commitment, comparable to the action of these two brothers in cutting loose from their present pattern of loyalties (these would be over-ridden; they would not be needlessly destroyed) and linking their lives with Christ himself.

We are now in a position to see the sequence of steps by which a man becomes a follower of Christ. They are not rules by which God is bound to act, but they do in fact describe the experience of many (as they describe the pattern followed in these verses). In their proper order, would you list these three steps as:

Repentance, faith, commitment?   **page 62**
Faith, repentance, commitment?   **page 51**
Commitment, repentance, faith?   **page 54**

From page 66

Your answer is that the reference to 'knowing Christ' in John 17.3 means a knowledge that comes from a response to His call.

This is perfectly correct. If you are in any doubt about the distinction between mere knowledge of the facts (knowing *about* a person) and the sort of knowledge spoken of in this verse (*knowing* a person by encounter and acquaintance and friendship) it may help you to look at pages 68 and 71.

* * *

For many readers, that is the end of the book. It set out to answer the question, 'What makes a man a Christian?', and it has tried to show, from our Lord's own calling of two of His disciples, and from the teaching of the New Testament, that what makes a man a Christian is knowing Jesus Christ in a personal way—in encounter and experience.

And we have seen that the steps by which men can come to know Him in this way begin with repentance, and continue through faith in, and personal commitment to, the living Christ Himself.

Other readers (and it is for them this book is really written) may not want to leave the matter there. For them, the form of the all-important question changes. It is not now, 'What makes a man a Christian?' but 'How can I become a Christian?' We use this question to begin a new chapter.

CHAPTER SEVEN

CHRIST AND MYSELF

WHICH SEEMS TO YOU the best of these three answers to the question, 'How can I become a Christian?'

By living the best life I can? **page 63**
By an encounter with Christ Himself? **page 67**
By learning more about Jesus Christ? **page 72**

61

From page 65

Your answer is that when Jesus called Simon and Andrew to follow Him, He told them that He wished to give them something.

No, this is not the right answer.

It is certainly true that Jesus wished to give these disciples many things—forgiveness, peace with God, a new joy in living—but it was not these gifts that He Himself chose to speak about at the time that He was calling them.

Go back to page 65 and try again

62

From page 59

Your answer is that the proper order of the three steps to Christ we have been considering is repentance, faith, commitment.

You are perfectly right. It should not have been a difficult question if you have been following the argument of this book so far. For the sake of those who chose a wrong answer first time, and to make sure that your right answer was based on more than luck, here is the reason.

Repentance must normally come first. It came first in our Lord's own sermon (Mark 1.15). No one is likely to bother with commands to believe the Gospel until they have begun to see how much they need it. Then they will listen and respond—and so faith (an active belief) comes second.

And commitment comes third because it springs from the first two. A simple illustration is the medical one. When my symptoms tell me that all is not well, and I recognize that I am sick and in need (repentance), then I am ready to hear the good news of a surgeon who can help me (believe the Gospel). And when I am convinced he knows his business, and can really help me—when, as we say, I 'have faith in him'—this faith will lead me to *commit* myself to his care—and to lie down on his operating table !

We have seen that the Bible does not use the word 'commitment', though the thought is continually present. But the idea of such commitment is implied in one of the common titles used for our Lord in the pages of the New Testament.

Do you find the idea of commitment most clearly implied in Christ's title :

'The Lord Jesus Christ' (Acts 11.17)?   **page 65**
'The Saviour of the World' (John 4.42)?   **page 52**
The 'Son of God' (Romans 1.4)?   **page 57**

63

From page 60

Your answer is that the way to become a Christian is by living the best life you can.

No. This is to put the cart before the horse. This is very like the answer that the policeman gave to Dr. Gallup's enquiry, in the first chapter of this book; and on page 12 you will find some of the reasons why this is not the right answer.

But the fact that you chose it is important. A great many people find it hard to believe that we cannot become Christians by our own efforts. The Anglo-Saxon race, especially, feel that the way to obtain anything is to earn it—but the Bible is very clear on this point: that there is nothing we can do to earn God's forgiveness. There is no way in which we can deserve Christ's offer to receive us and be our Saviour and Lord. Here are some words from Ephesians 2 : 'For it is by his grace you are saved, through trusting him; it is not your own doing. It is God's gift, not a reward for work done.' Of *course* when a man is a Christian, he will try to live the best life he can. But no amount of his own efforts will ever make him a Christian. Only God can do that; and He chooses to do it as a gift, imparted through the knowledge of His Son, Jesus Christ.

Go back to page 60 and try again

64

From page 69

Your answer is that by the words 'eternal life' the Bible means primarily life of an endless duration.

No, it does not primarily mean that. Eternal life, as far as we know, will be of an endless duration, if those words have meaning outside the scale of earthly time. Indeed, in the Bible, an alternative name for it is 'everlasting life'. But its duration is by no means the most important thing about it.

Here is a clue that may help you to do better in your second choice: in St. John's Gospel, chapter 17, verse 3, in a prayer to His Father, Jesus gives us a definition of 'eternal life'. You may like to look at it before making another attempt.

When you are ready, go back to page 69 and try again

65

From page 62

Your answer is that you find the idea of commitment most clearly implied in the title 'The Lord Jesus Christ'.

I agree. It is possible to read the idea of commitment into both the other titles (you will find this indicated on pages 52 and 57 respectively) but it is most clearly seen in the description of Jesus as 'The Lord'. Not only is this the word used by the New Testament on many occasions to refer to God the Father (as in Matthew 1.20 when 'an angel of the Lord' appeared to Joseph), but it is the ordinary Greek word for 'Master', and is so used, for instance, by Jesus Christ in His famous saying about 'No servant can be slave to two masters' (Matthew 6.24).

The word 'slave' gives us a further clue. In the days when the New Testament was written, it would be hard to find a better or more clear-cut example of total commitment than the commitment of a slave to his owner or master. True, it was not always a willing commitment, but it was effectual, total, and extending to every aspect of life. St. Paul takes over this whole picture of the relation of slave to master, and applies it to Christian discipleship. He proudly calls himself 'a servant of Jesus Christ' (e.g. Romans 1.1.; Philippians 1.1.), using the word that in ordinary Greek meant 'slave'. When, therefore, we speak of Jesus Christ as LORD, it reminds us that what He asks is commitment and obedience.

Without looking back to check, recall to your mind the invitation of Christ to Simon and Andrew, the two fishermen with the net. When He asked them to follow Him, did He tell them that He wished:

To teach them something?	page 58
To make them something?	page 69
To give them something?	page 61

66

From page 69

Your answer is that by the words 'eternal life', the Bible means primarily life of a spiritual quality.

Correct. This life is not cut short by death, and is therefore sometimes spoken of in the Bible as 'everlasting life'. It certainly continues in heaven. But primarily the words 'eternal life' speak of life with an eternal quality about it—spiritual life. In one place our Lord spoke of it as life 'in all its fullness' (John 10.10).

You may recall that right at the start of this book, when we were still considering Dr. Gallup's survey, we suggested that the essential key to what makes a man a Christian was not found in ceremonies, or codes, or creeds, but (page 18) in spiritual life. And we added, 'The secret of Christianity—the secret of spiritual life—lies in Jesus Christ Himself'. He makes this very plain in His own great prayer to the Father in John 17.3: 'This is eternal life: to know thee who alone art truly God, and Jesus Christ whom thou hast sent.'

Commitment to Christ, then, as Saviour from our sins and Lord of our lives, follows from repentance and faith. Committed to Him, we find in knowing Him this new quality of life, the vital spark. Without it, religious observances and good deeds and ortho-dox beliefs are like dead sticks and black coals in a grate. When it is linked with repentance and faith, commitment brings the living fire that sets the whole ablaze. This is what makes a man a Christian.

Look again at John 17.3, quoted above. Does this reference to 'knowing Christ' mean a knowledge that comes:

From a response to His call? **page 60**
From a study of the Scriptures? **page 68**
From a reverent familiarity with the facts of His life
and death? **page 71**

67

From page 60

Your answer is that the way to become a Christian is by an encounter with Christ Himself.

Yes, this is perfectly right. And if *you* are to become a Christian, in the New Testament sense of the word, you need to meet with Christ, to encounter Him, to respond to His invitation. You need to trace in your own experience the three steps with which this book has been concerned, of

> Repentance
> Belief
> Commitment

and to begin with *repentance*.

You will see that this has suddenly ceased to be an impersonal enquiry, a mere search for knowledge (as though this were a book about mathematics). It has become a personal matter, in which you are faced with a decision. I appeal to you to treat it seriously in choosing which of the sentences below most clearly expresses your own position.

Faced with the first step of personal repentance, is your position:

I am ready to repent and would like to know how?   **page 70**
I have had enough, and am not prepared for this to become a personal matter?   **page 83**
I am still not clear what repentance means?   **page 75**

68

From page 66

Your answer is that the reference to 'knowing Christ' in John 17.3 means a knowledge that comes from a study of the Scriptures.

No, it cannot just mean that.

When our Lord spoke these words, in the hearing of His first disciples, not a word of the New Testament was written. And though we today are dependent on the Scriptures for all we know (in any detail) of the Lord Jesus Christ, yet this verse is referring to knowledge of a more intimate kind than can come by simply reading about Him. When it comes, it may well be based on what we have come to know *about* Christ from reading the Bible. But it will not be *knowing about* any longer—it will be knowing. You can see the difference if you think, for instance, of the Prime Minister. Most readers of this book will know quite a lot about the Prime Minister, from newspapers and television, and perhaps from having seen him on a number of occasions. But few will be able to claim that they know him personally, and enjoy his acquaintance, in the way we know our intimate friends. Jesus did not imply that eternal life came by knowing *about* Him—but by personal, intimate acquaintance.

Go back to page 66 and try again

69

From page 65

Your answer is that when Jesus called Simon and Andrew to follow Him, He told them that He wished to make them something.

Correct; and I have no doubt you could add what it was He wished to make of them—fishers of men.

It is of course true (though He did not choose that moment to speak of it) that Jesus wanted to teach them many things (there is a word about this on page 58) and to give them many things (page 61). But when He called them to commit themselves to Him and follow Him, it was because His plan for their lives included *making something of them*. He had a purpose for them; a job for them to do. He would equip and commission them for new work.

This, too, is part of what commitment means for us, when we are called to follow Christ. He will accept us as we are, but He will not be content with us as we are. If He is the Master (Lord) and we the servant (or slave) then true commitment means total obedience—that *what He says goes*! Or, as Paul puts it in his letter to the Christians at Corinth: 'You do not belong to yourselves; you were bought at a price' (1 Corinthians 6.20).

At first sight, such total commitment looks to us like death—the submerging of our own freedom, will, and personality. In fact, because it brings us, not into casual contact, but into living touch with Christ, it marks the start of a new life—life of a new quality or dimension altogether, often spoken of in the Bible as 'eternal life' (e.g. John 3.15).

By the words 'eternal life' do you suppose the Bible means primarily:

Life after death, in heaven?   **page 55**

Life of a spiritual quality?   **page 66**

Life of an endless duration?   **page 64**

From page 67

Your position is that, faced with the step of personal repentance, you are ready to repent and would like to know how.

Good. These simple numbered steps may be useful as a guide :*

1. Kneel down. Never mind if you feel a fool. Let this be a sign that you are in earnest in your search for Christ.
2. Ask God to help you. Tell Him (out loud if you like) that you are taking seriously His command to repent.
3. Go carefully over your past life. Think, if they come to your mind, of individual sins, but more especially of the whole trend and tenor of your living. Take just the two great commandments that Jesus spoke of, and measure your life by them :

> 'Love the Lord your God with all your heart . . . Love your neighbour as yourself' (Mark 12.30).

Have you kept, consistently, even these two commandments?
4. Confess your sins to God. Tell Him that you do not hide from Him anything you have ever said or done or been.
5. Turn your thoughts to the future. Recognize that mere good resolutions are not enough. Tell God that, as best you know, you want a change of heart. Say to Him, and mean it, 'I now repent.'

If all this is empty words, you will know and God will know. But if even some of it is genuine, and heartfelt, God will know that too. This *is* repentance. After repentance comes belief. Faced with the step of personal belief in Christ, is your position :

I am ready to believe. Tell me what to do?   **page 76**
I have had enough, and do not wish to go further?   **page 83**
I am still not clear what 'belief' means?   **page 73**

---

* You may prefer to read to the end of the book first, to get a clear picture of the steps involved. Then you can return to this page, and trace them in your own experience.

71

From page 66

Your answer is that the reference to 'knowing Christ' in John 17.3 means a knowledge that comes from a reverent familiarity with the facts of His life and death.

No, this is not right.

A familiarity with the facts, however reverent, is *knowledge about*, and a different thing entirely from personal acquaintance. Comparatively recently, the word 'encounter' has been popular to describe what happens when we enter into a living contact with Christ Himself. You can see from the use of that word that to *know about* someone, in the sense of familiarity with the facts of his life, is the work simply of our mind. It is head-knowledge. But to know someone, in the sense of *encounter*—to know them as we know our intimate friends—is not just a matter of our minds and heads, but of our whole persons, and not least our hearts!

Our Lord, in John 17.3, is talking of a knowledge deeper than any unaided study of the facts can secure—for a computer might marshal the facts more reliably and accurately than we could do ourselves, but no computer is in the running for eternal life!

Go back to page 66 and try again

72

From page 60

Your answer is that the way to become a Christian is by learning more about Jesus Christ.

No, this may be an essential preliminary, but it is not the heart of the matter. There are enemies of Christianity who, to try and destroy it, have made a close study of the life of Jesus Christ, but all their learning about Him has not made them Christians.

Your answer falls into the very popular trap of confusing *knowing about* and *knowing* (personally, as we know our friends). No amount of *learning more about* is going to make you a Christian—though it may help you in your search for a personal encounter with Jesus Christ. You will find the difference between *knowing* and *knowing about* explained more fully on pages 68 and 71.

When you are ready, go back to page 60 and try again

73

From page 70

Your position is that, faced with the step of personal belief in Christ, you are still not clear what belief means.

Your confusion may spring from a number of causes:

1. When we originally met the command to 'believe', in our Lord's first sermon in Galilee (you will find it on page 29) it was in the words 'believe the Gospel'. If you are not clear What 'the Gospel' is then go back to page 29, and follow the argument from there, until you feel your confusion has been dealt with, or your memory jogged.

2. But your difficulty may be that, while Jesus said, 'Believe the Gospel', the words at the head of this page talk of 'belief in Christ'. There is a purpose in this. We tend to think that 'Believe the Gospel' means 'Assent to the facts'; and for that reason I chose the words 'belief in Christ'. You will probably recall easily enough the fact that our Lord was *not* asking for a mere intellectual assent by returning to page 46 and following the argument from there until you feel your problem has been answered.

3. If neither of the paragraphs above accurately describe the cause of your difficulty, then you might be well advised to go over carefully the whole of the section in this book dealing with 'belief', which begins on page 29.

4. If this still leaves you uncertain, then I suggest you shelve your problem for a moment, and adopt the position described on page 70 as, 'I am ready to believe. Tell me what to do.' You will find there some practical help which may solve your difficulty.

When you are ready, go back to page 70 and see if your position has changed, and you are ready to go forward

Your position is, that faced with the final step of personal commitment to Christ, you are ready to commit yourself and would like to know how.

Good. I think I can help you.

The easiest example of commitment between persons is probably a wedding. At a marriage ceremony the man declares that he will take the woman to be his wife—'to have and to hold from this day forward, for better for worse, for richer for poorer, in sickness and in health . . . till death us do part.' By this promise he *commits* himself to her, and she by a similar promise commits herself to him.

This is a good picture of what happens when Christ calls us to be His followers, as He called Simon and Andrew in Galilee with the words, 'Come with me, and I will make you fishers of men.' His call today comes to us in many different ways—it may come to you through the reading of this book. It is up to you to answer, and you say (if your own position is in fact the one described at the top of the page) that you are ready to respond.

Kneel down, then, and tell Jesus Christ that in answer to His call, you are at this moment coming to Him to be His follower. 'Come' was an invitation He was constantly giving—'Come to me' or 'Come with me'. And just as the act of repentance was marked by telling God 'I do repent', and the act of believing by telling God 'I do believe', so the act of commitment asked of you is to tell God 'I come'—and mean it. It is as simple as that. Ask any couple, and they will tell you there is nothing complicated about actually getting married. It can be done in less than half-an-hour. But when they leave the church, *committed to one another*, their whole life is changed—though they will not realize all that marriage means for a long time to come.

So you. When you rise from your knees, you may feel that nothing tremendous has occurred. But if you meant what you said to God, it is the start of a new life. Whether you feel like it or not, however little you know of what may be involved, you WILL BE A CHRISTIAN.

Here are two choices. If you are ready to kneel down and tell

Continued at the foot of page 75 opposite

75

From page 67

Your position is, that faced with the step of personal repentance, you are still not clear what repentance means.

This is not surprising—we have had a good many things to consider in this book since last we were dealing with the meaning of repentance. You will find the section on this subject begins on page 22 of this book, and if you will go back and follow the argument (by answering the questions) from there, you will not have to read many pages before you have completed your 'revision' on the meaning of repentance.

And you will in fact find some more practical help on the page to which you are referred when you are ready to choose (on page 67) the position: 'I am ready to repent and would like to know how.'

When you are ready, go back to page 67 and see if your position has changed, and you are ready to go forward

---

Continued from page 74 opposite

Christ in your own words that you do repent of your sin, you do believe He died to save you, and now at this moment you do come to Him in answer to His call, then do just that. Never mind books now. This is the real thing.

But if you would like to see (and perhaps use, as long as you really mean it) a prayer which tells God all this, simply and clearly, then you will find one on page 77.   **page 77**

Afterwards, you can take up this book again and read the last chapter.   **page 80**

Your position is, that faced with the step of personal belief in Christ, you are ready to believe and would like to know how.

Good. This is the second step which our Lord asked of His hearers in that first sermon in Galilee. The command to *believe* followed hard on the heels of His call to them to repent. On this page, therefore, we build on the foundation of your personal repentance.

1. When you say you are ready to believe, I assume by this that you accept the New Testament record. I cannot give you any simple instructions about how to believe something contrary to your convictions! This page is concerned to explain just how, in an immediate and practical way, you can take the step of *putting your faith in Jesus Christ.* If you lack all conviction on the facts of Christianity I have only one suggestion to make: in his letter to the Christians at Rome, Paul told them of the source from which faith springs: 'Faith is awakened by the message, and the message that awakens it comes through the word of Christ' (Romans 10.17). Your attention, therefore, should be given to reading 'the message' and 'the word of Christ'—which for us means the New Testament.

2. But I take it that you do not deny any of what this book has set before you. Rather, at this moment, you want to obey Christ's command to believe. You can do this in much the same way as you obeyed His command to repent—by telling him, in prayer, that you do obey Him. Kneel down, and think through in your mind what the New Testament tells us of the death and resurrection of our Lord. Recall that He died 'for our sins'—which means as far as you are now concerned, for *your* sins. Think how futile would be your repentance if there was no way by which the past could be put right. And then tell God that you *do* believe that Christ's costly, painful death was for *your* sins. Tell Him that you *do* believe that Christ rose from the grave, having conquered death and hell, and is alive for evermore. Tell God that you *do* believe Him to be able, through the Gospel, to meet every need of your soul.

In a word, just as repentance is confessing to God that you are

Continued at the foot of page 77 opposite

From page 74

You asked for a prayer, putting into words what you want to say to God about repenting of your sins, believing Christ died to save you, and being ready now to come to Him.

Here is such a prayer. The words don't matter at all. Use them if it helps (as long as you really mean them) or use your own.

LORD JESUS, I admit I am a sinner, and I have sinned many times in thought, word and deed. I am sorry for my sins, and I turn from them in repentance.
I believe that you died on the cross for my sins, to make possible my forgiveness. Thank you for what you have done.
And now I come to you, and commit myself to you. Make what you will of my life. Take me as I am, and teach me to live for you as a Christian from this day forward. Amen.

When you have prayed such a prayer as this, telling God of your repentance, belief and commitment, you will yourself have become a Christian.

Now read the final chapter on page 80

Continued from page 76 opposite

a needy sinner, so believing is affirming to God that you know Christ can meet that need. If that is your position, now is the time to act.* You will then stand on the brink of the third and final step, which is commitment. Look again at three different sentences, and choose the one which most clearly expresses your own position.

I am ready to commit myself to Christ, please tell
me what to do?   **page 74**
I have had enough, and do not wish to go further   **page 83**
I am still not clear what 'commitment to Christ' means **page 79**

* You may prefer to read to the end of the book first, to get a clear picture of all the steps involved. Then you can return (to page 70) and trace them in your own experience.

From page 80

Your answer is, No, it does not matter whether or not I feel any different immediately I have become a Christian.

You are quite right. It does not matter at all. Feelings are unreliable and changing guides. Christ's promise *never to turn away* those who answer His call is secure and unchanging. Trust His promise, and never mind what you feel. If you *do* feel different, thank God for it, but do not trust your new feeling — trust the promise of Christ. If you feel no different at all, this is not a let-down. Again, trust Christ's promise, and thank Him that you can be sure beyond all doubt that He has made you welcome. Have no doubts that you are now His disciple, with your sins forgiven, and with the gift of eternal life.

And this brings us nearly to the end of this book, and to the last question : Which of these two better expresses what you regard as your own position now :

Having at last become a Christian, I have come to
the end of a long road   **page 81**
Having at last become a Christian, I have set my feet
on the start of a long road   **page 84**

From page 76

Your position is, that faced with the step of personal commitment to Christ, you are still not clear what commitment means.

You have done the right thing by turning to this page, because if you are not clear, the best thing to do is to say so ! It is some way back in this book that we considered the subject of commitment, and it will probably help you best to go back and re-read that section. It will not take you long, answering the questions and moving on to the pages referred to, because you will not have many misconceptions to clear up—so the number of pages you actually read will be drastically reduced. You had best begin reading at chapter five, PROGRESS REPORT, on page 49. When you are clearer in your mind about the meaning of commitment to Christ, then you may find one of the other sentences on page 76 fits you better. And even if you are still not fully clear, it may be best to shelve your problem for the moment, and turn to the page indicated against the words, 'I am ready to commit myself to Christ. Please tell me what to do.' Quite possibly that page itself will clear up your difficulty.

When you are ready, go back to page 76 and see if your position has changed, and you are ready to move forward

CHAPTER EIGHT

A NEW LIFE

IF, AS BEST YOU KNOW, you have taken the three steps to Christ of repentance, belief and commitment, then, whether you feel it or not, *you are now a Christian*. You have begun a new life.

You may well find this hard to realize. It may even be that you are full of doubts: 'Am I good enough?' you may be asking. Jesus never asked that about anyone. He called, and accepted those who came. 'Suppose when I came to Him, He was not willing to accept me? How can I be sure that He has?' is a very common question. And there are several very faulty answers to it, and one undeniable answer. It is this. 'You can be sure, *because Jesus promised*.'

Look at John 6.37, to choose only one among many examples. There Jesus Christ said without qualification: 'All that the Father gives me will come to me, and the man who comes to me I will never turn away.' Do you believe that He means what He says? Of course you do! Have you come to Him as he asks? Yes, as best you know, you have, if you have prayed the sort of prayer suggested on page 77 or 74. Well then, there can be only one answer to the question. 'Did He welcome you as His follower, or did He turn you away? HE WELCOMED YOU AS HE PROMISED.

Once you are sure of that, thank Him again, in your own words, and tell Him that you *know* He has welcomed you and that you are His follower.

Many people, when they have just become Christians, expect in some way to feel different. It may help you to answer the following question: Does it matter whether you feel different or not?

Yes   page 82

No   page 78

From page 78

Your own position is now summed up by saying, 'Having at last become a Christian, I have come to the end of a long road.'

This is true, and there is no harm in saying it.

Just as the birth of Christ divides the history of the world, and we talk of dates as BC or AD, so when we commit ourselves to Him and become His followers, that marks a radical division in our life. What has gone before, in the purpose of God, has been preparing for this moment. There are some things we shall look back on with satisfaction and affection—as well as blacker bits that are now dealt with and forgiven—but today marks the start of a new life.

The new Christian's eyes, then, should be on the future—the other alternative offered on page 78 expressed it like this: 'Having at last become a Christian, I have set my feet *on the start* of a long road.' You cannot now stand still. You must begin to reorganize your life, as a disciple of Christ.

Go back to page 78 and adopt the other position

82

From page 80

Your answer is, Yes, it does matter whether or not I feel any different immediately I have become a Christian.

No, in fact it does not matter at all. This is the wrong answer. Our feelings are very unreliable guides—and they are especially unreliable about our spiritual state. Some people do rise from their knees, having committed themselves to Christ for ever, with a glowing consciousness that they are really beginning a new life. 'I feel different already,' they say. If you feel like that, fine. I am glad that you do. *But it is really not important.* What is important is that you should not rely on any experience of 'feeling different' as evidence that you really are a Christian. Tomorrow the feeling may have left you. Will that mean you are no longer a Christian? Of course not. Your acceptance as Christ's follower stands on His own unshakable promise, which will be the same tomorrow as it is today. If you are in doubt about this, re-read carefully what is said on page 80 before choosing another answer.

On the other hand, you may feel totally unchanged. This also is quite unimportant. Cling to *the fact of Christ's promise.* In the face of that word, 'The man who comes to me I will never turn away', can you really believe that He has *not* welcomed you and made you His follower? Given time, you probably will come to 'feel differently'—His peace and joy will make themselves felt within you. But whatever your feelings, HIS PROMISE STANDS.

Go back to page 80 and try again

83

From page 67 or page 70 or page 76

Your position is, that as you learn more of what it will mean to become a Christian, you want to call a halt, and are not prepared for this to become a personal matter.

It is your decision.

In a way, too, it is a very familiar one. A good many people who have been interested in Christianity cool off at once as soon as it seems that Christ Himself may have claims upon their own lives. He never suggested that it would be easy to follow Him. If you are determined to drop the matter now, then for you, this book ends here.

But I would like to say this: it may never be easier to go forward with Christian discipleship than it is now. The Bible is full of sayings which remind us that God has times and seasons, and that we cannot rely on His call returning to us, if we dismiss it when it comes. The writer to the Hebrews quotes God the Holy Spirit as saying to us: 'Today if you hear his voice, do not grow stubborn.'

And I would remind you that eternal issues are involved. In the hour of death and in the day of judgment, only Christ can help. Before you finish this final page, search your reasons for refusing to allow this matter to go further. Tell God your motives and ask His help in dealing with them. Ask yourself if it will solve any problem, or make you any happier, to refuse to listen to Christ's call.

You may remember the man in the story who wanted to follow Jesus—until he learned what it would cost. 'When the young man heard this,' Matthew tells us, 'he went away with a heavy heart; for he was a man of great wealth.' Weigh those words *'with a heavy heart'*. No one ever went *gladly away* from Jesus Christ. Not, I suspect, even you.

But, as I say, it is your decision. Look at the alternatives set out below. Which will you choose?

I still do not want to face the personal challenge of Christian discipleship **page . . . but there are no more pages for you**
I am willing to suspend judgment, and learn more.

Go back to pages 67, 70 or 76, whichever you read last

84

From page 78

Your own position is summed up by saying, 'Having at last become a Christian, I have set my feet on the start of a long road.'

You have indeed, and it is good to recognize it clearly. For while you may like to regard this milestone in your life as marking the end of an era, the Bible speaks of it as marking a beginning. It says, indeed, that to become a Christian is like being born as a baby—or as J. B. Phillips puts it, 'If a man is in Christ he becomes a new person altogether—the past is finished and gone, everything has become fresh and new' (2 Corinthians 5.17).

Now, therefore, you will start to re-shape your life as a disciple of Jesus Christ. If you have not been baptized you will want Christian baptism. You will want to join a church (make sure it is a live one, and not a dead one!) and meet other Christians. You will want to find time in your day for prayer, and for reading the Bible. You may be able to get hold of some of the books and booklets mentioned on the next page, and start learning more of this new life you have begun. You will want to consider practical ways in which, as Christ's disciple, you can serve your generation.

But there is one thing to do first. Tell somebody that you have become a Christian. This is what Christ Himself asked of His friends (Matthew 10.32). If this book was put into your hands by a Christian friend, tell him. If you already attend a church (lots of people do, who are not yet Christians) then tell your minister. If you are married, tell your partner. But tell someone. However halting your words, or pink your face, these first words of testimony as a true follower of Christ will be a great step forward.

And may God bless you in your new life for Him.*

---

* If you have read this book to the end, before starting to tell God of your own repentance, belief and commitment, then turn back now to page 70 and begin to make what you have just been reading about a reality in your own experience.

WHAT TO READ NEXT

Basic Christianity by *J. R. W. Stott*, I.V.F.
The Way by *Godfrey Robinson and Stephen Winward*,
   Scripture Union
Christian Living by *R. J. B. Eddison*, Scripture Union
Your Confirmation by *J. R. W. Stott*, Hodder and Stoughton
Finding the Answer by *G. R. Harding Wood*, Falcon Books

   (All the above are available as paperbacks.)

On page 84 of this book there is a reference to daily Bible reading.
No single habit, carefully cultivated, will help a new Christian
as much as this one. For a tested method of daily Bible reading,
including notes suitable for those with no previous experience of
reading the Bible, you are advised to write to The Scripture Union,
5 Wigmore Street, London W.1., mentioning this book.